# Say Hi To Your Riches:

## And Bid farewell to financial difficulties

By

Daniel J. Buttler

Copyright © 2023 by Daniel J. Buttler All rights reserved. This book or any portion thereof may not be reproduced or used in any manner whatsoever without the express written permission of the publisher except for the use of brief quotations in a book review.

# Disclaimer

This book is intended solely for educational and informational purposes and should not be considered as financial or investment advice. The author is not a financial advisor and the strategies and ideas presented may not be suitable for every individual. It is recommended that readers conduct their own research and consult with a qualified financial advisor before making any investment decisions. The author and publisher cannot be held liable for any losses or damages incurred as a result of the information provided in this book. The success stories and examples provided are not a guarantee of future success and the accuracy, completeness, reliability, or suitability of the information cannot be guaranteed. The reader assumes all risks associated with the use of this information and the author and publisher will not be held responsible for any damages that may arise from the use of this book or the information provided.

# Table of Content

Introduction

Chapter 1: Assessing Your Financial Situation

Chapter 2: Building Wealth Through Savings and Investments

Chapter 3: Building Multiple Streams of Income

Chapter 4: Overcoming Financial Obstacles

Chapter 5: Building a Wealth Mindset

Conclusion: Say Hi to Your Riches!

## Introduction:

If you're ready to turn your financial dreams into reality, then let's get started and begin building your wealth today! This book is an essential resource for anyone who wants to learn practical techniques and proven strategies for building wealth and achieving financial freedom. Whether you're starting your financial journey or looking to take your wealth-building efforts to the next level, this book provides insights and tools to help you succeed. The book covers a wide range of topics, including establishing a strong financial foundation, managing debt, budgeting, and saving. It also explores the world of investing, examining various investment options and long-term growth strategies. The book is written in a clear and concise manner, making it easy to understand and apply the concepts discussed. Throughout the book, you'll find practical tips and real-life examples that can help you put the strategies into action and achieve success.

Furthermore, financial freedom is not just about personal benefits. It also has broader societal implications. When individuals are financially free, they are less likely to rely on government assistance programs, reducing the strain on public resources. Additionally, financially free individuals are more likely to contribute to the economy through spending, investment, and job creation. In conclusion, financial freedom is a critical component of a fulfilling and successful life. It provides individuals with the ability to pursue their passions, make positive contributions to society, and achieve their long-term goals. By prioritizing financial freedom, individuals can create a more secure and prosperous future for themselves and those around them. Being financially free means having the ability to pay off debts, save for the future, invest in oneself, and enjoy the fruits of one's labor. It means being able to take risks and pursue one's passions without fear of financial ruin. It also means having the power to make a positive impact on the world by supporting causes and organizations that align with one's values. In contrast, being financially constrained can lead to stress, anxiety, and limited opportunities. Living paycheck to paycheck or being burdened by debt can make it difficult to focus on personal growth and professional development. It can also limit one's ability to pursue opportunities that may require financial investment, such as starting a business or pursuing further education.

# Chapter 1

## Assessing Your Financial Situation

To effectively evaluate your financial status, you must conduct a thorough analysis of your financial situation. This entails examining your revenue streams, expenditure patterns, possessions, and debts. It is a crucial stage in attaining financial stability as it serves as the groundwork for developing a sound financial strategy. When evaluating your financial situation, there are several important actions to consider in order to gain a comprehensive picture of your financial health.

Calculate your present earnings: This encompasses all forms of income, including your occupation, investments, rental proceeds, and any other sources of financial inflow.

Take the time to carefully assess and determine the total amount of money you spend on a regular basis by creating a comprehensive and detailed breakdown of both your static and fluctuating expenditures. This should encompass a wide range of categories such as housing costs, food expenses, transportation fees, entertainment expenditures, as well as any other miscellaneous or additional outlays you may have.

When assessing your financial situation, it is important to consider all of your valuable possessions, including your house, vehicle, savings, and retirement funds. These are all assets that can contribute to your overall net worth and financial stability.

Assess your financial obligations: This encompasses any outstanding debts that you are responsible for, including but not limited to credit card debt, loans taken for educational purposes, and mortgage loans.

Your financial standing can be evaluated by calculating your net worth, which is achieved by deducting all your liabilities from your assets. This provides you with a summary of your present financial situation. It is important to identify areas where you can make improvements in your financial situation. This can include finding ways to lower your expenses, increasing your income, and paying off any outstanding debts. By doing this, you can develop a clear plan for reaching your financial goals and improving your overall financial well-being.

Continuously evaluating and adjusting your financial situation is a crucial and ongoing process that should not be overlooked. Through careful examination of your financial status, you can develop a detailed plan to attain financial prosperity and establish sustainable wealth over the long run.

Assessing your financial situation goes beyond just looking at your income and expenses. It's about looking at your finances holistically and understanding your overall financial health. Here are some additional factors to consider when assessing your financial situation:

Cash flow is a financial concept that refers to the amount of money that comes in and goes out of your accounts or business. It is the difference between the money you earn and the money you spend on various expenses. Knowing your cash flow is crucial since it allows you to pinpoint the areas in which you can cut costs or increase revenue. By analyzing your cash flow, you can determine whether you have enough money to cover your expenses and make informed decisions about saving, investing, and budgeting. In short, understanding your cash flow is essential for financial planning and achieving your long-term financial goals. In order to attain financial success, it is essential to prioritize saving money. By carefully evaluating the amount that you are able to save, you can effectively determine if you are on track to reaching your financial objectives. Debt is a significant hurdle in attaining financial prosperity. Evaluating the extent of your debt will enable you to gauge whether you need to implement measures to decrease your debt and curtail interest charges.

An emergency fund is a type of savings account that serves as a financial cushion for unexpected expenses that may arise. It is crucial to evaluate the sufficiency of your emergency fund because it acts as a safety net in case of unforeseen circumstances such as losing your job, falling ill, or needing major repairs. Having an adequate emergency fund can provide peace of mind and help minimize the financial impact of unexpected events.

Evaluating your retirement savings is a crucial step in ensuring that you are on course to achieve your retirement objectives. This involves examining your present retirement account balances and forecasting your future retirement income requirements. By doing so, you can determine if you need to adjust your savings strategy to meet your retirement goals.

Through a thorough examination of your financial status, you can obtain a complete comprehension of your financial well-being and pinpoint areas where there is room for improvement. This will enable you to formulate a strategy for attaining your financial objectives and establishing sustainable prosperity in the long run.

## Chapter 2

## Building Wealth Through Savings and Investments

To achieve financial success, it's important to focus on building wealth through savings and investments. There are several effective strategies for doing so, which we'll explore in greater detail below.

Establishing financial objectives is a crucial step in the process of saving and investing. It involves delineating both short-term aspirations, such as creating a safety net for unexpected expenses, and long-term aspirations, such as accumulating funds for retirement or purchasing a property.

Developing a budget is an effective way to carefully monitor the inflow and outflow of your finances, enabling you to gain a comprehensive understanding of your income and expenses. By meticulously examining your financial situation, you can identify various areas where you can potentially decrease your spending and enhance your savings. This can involve implementing tactics like reducing unnecessary expenditures, engaging in negotiations to secure lower bills, and exploring alternative avenues to generate additional income.

Creating a financial safety net in the form of an emergency fund is paramount in the journey towards financial prosperity. This specially designated savings account acts as a protective cushion, shielding you from the financial aftermath of unforeseen circumstances such as exorbitant medical bills, unexpected car repairs, or even the untimely loss of employment. By diligently accumulating funds in this emergency fund, you are equipping yourself with the necessary tools to navigate through life's unpredictabilities without succumbing to the burdensome weight of debt. To make the most of your retirement savings, it is recommended that you take advantage of retirement accounts like 401(k) or IRA by contributing the maximum amount allowed. These accounts provide tax benefits and the potential for compound interest, allowing your savings to grow significantly in the long run.

On the other hand, bonds provide a more stable investment option. Bonds are essentially loans made to governments or corporations, where you, as an investor, lend a certain amount of money for a fixed period of time and, in return, receive periodic interest payments and the full amount of your initial investment at maturity. While the returns on bonds tend to be lower compared to stocks, they also come with a lower level of risk. This is because bonds are generally considered a safer investment due to the contractual nature of the borrower's obligation to repay the principal and interest. Determining the right investment strategy that aligns with your financial goals and risk tolerance can be a complex task. It is advisable to seek guidance from a financial advisor who can help you navigate the intricacies of the stock and bond markets. A financial advisor will consider factors such as your financial situation, investment goals, and risk appetite to develop a tailored investment plan that maximizes returns while minimizing potential risks. In conclusion, investing in stocks and bonds can be a fruitful endeavor for long-term wealth accumulation. While stocks offer the potential for higher returns, they also come with a higher level of risk. Bonds, on the other hand, provide stability and lower risk but tend to offer lower returns. Working with a financial advisor can be immensely beneficial in developing an investment strategy that suits your specific needs and allows you to make informed decisions in the world of stocks and bonds. When it comes to stocks, they offer the allure of potentially higher returns compared to other investment avenues. This is primarily because stocks represent ownership in a company, and as the company grows and becomes more profitable, the value of your stock can increase. However, it is important to remember that higher returns also mean higher risk. The stock market can be volatile, and the value of your stocks can fluctuate significantly, sometimes even drastically. Therefore, it is essential to thoroughly research and analyze the companies you are considering investing in to mitigate potential risks. Investing in stocks and bonds can be a wise decision when it comes to building long-term wealth. By allocating your funds towards these investment options, you open up the potential for significant returns on your investment. However, it is crucial to understand that stocks and bonds come with their own set of characteristics and risk factors that should be carefully considered before making any investment decisions.

Real estate investing can be a lucrative option for those looking to increase their wealth through property appreciation and rental income. However, it is important to acknowledge the potential risks involved and the financial commitment required. To make informed decisions, it is recommended to consult with a professional in the real estate industry who can provide expert advice and help evaluate potential investment opportunities.

In order to achieve a state of financial stability and independence, individuals must possess certain qualities such as self-discipline, determination, and a proactive approach towards saving and investing. By cultivating positive financial habits and taking advantage of various opportunities, individuals can steadily increase their wealth over a significant period of time. It is of utmost importance to remain committed to the process and acknowledge that success often necessitates a combination of patience and perseverance. Through consistently making wise choices and keeping sight of their long-term goals, individuals of all backgrounds can attain the desired state of financial autonomy and peace of mind.

Achieving financial success and building wealth is not a sprint, it's a marathon that requires a combination of discipline, patience, and a long-term perspective. The key to building wealth is to set realistic financial goals, create a budget, build an emergency fund, maximize retirement contributions, and invest in a diverse portfolio. These important steps will help you build long-term wealth and achieve financial success. By setting goals, you can prioritize your spending and saving habits, allowing you to create a plan to achieve your financial objectives. Building an emergency fund is essential for unexpected expenses, such as medical bills or car repairs, and will help you avoid dipping into your savings or retirement funds. Maximizing your retirement contributions will ensure that you are saving enough to support your future lifestyle, and investing in a diverse portfolio will minimize your risk and maximize your potential returns. In summary, building wealth requires dedication, planning, and a long-term perspective, but by taking these critical steps, you can achieve financial success and secure your financial future.

# Chapter 3
# Building Multiple Streams of Income

Another benefit of having multiple income streams is that it can increase your earning potential. With multiple streams, you have the opportunity to earn more money than you would with just one source. It also allows you to explore different career paths and side hustles that align with your skills and interests. Creating multiple income streams can also provide you with more financial freedom and flexibility. You can use the extra income to pay off debts, save for retirement, or invest in other ventures. Additionally, having multiple streams of income can allow you to pursue your passions and interests without worrying about the financial implications. In conclusion, having multiple income streams is essential for financial stability, flexibility, and security. It can increase your earning potential, provide you with more financial freedom, and reduce stress and anxiety about finances. Therefore, it is crucial to explore different income streams and find ways to diversify your sources of income. Furthermore, having multiple income streams can provide a sense of security and peace of mind. It can reduce stress and anxiety about finances, allowing you to focus on other areas of your life. It is essential to have multiple sources of income, and here are the reasons why. Having multiple income streams is crucial for financial stability and security. It allows you to diversify your sources of income, reducing the risk of relying solely on one source. In today's unpredictable economic climate, having a single source of income can be dangerous, as it can easily disappear in the event of a job loss or economic downturn.

Having multiple streams of income can bring various benefits to your financial life. Firstly, in the unfortunate circumstance of losing your primary income source, having supplementary income streams can provide stability and ease financial stress. Additionally, diversifying your income sources can help you accumulate wealth more quickly through the power of compounding. This can lead to greater financial security and the ability to achieve your financial goals sooner. To create additional income streams, there are various types to consider. These can include investing in stocks or real estate, starting a side business or freelancing, creating digital products or services, or even earning money through affiliate marketing or sponsored content. By exploring these options and finding the ones that align with your skills and interests, you can begin to build a diversified income portfolio and enjoy the benefits of multiple streams of income. Another advantage of having multiple streams of income is the flexibility and freedom it provides. With additional income sources, you have more options to choose work you enjoy and can be more selective in your career choices. Moreover, having multiple income streams can open up opportunities for generating passive income, allowing you to earn money while you sleep.

Active income refers to income that is earned through the direct involvement and active participation of an individual. This type of income requires one's time and effort, as it involves tasks such as freelancing, online tutoring, or driving for a ridesharing service. In other words, active income is the result of actively working and putting in the necessary effort to earn money. Lastly, portfolio income is derived from assets and investments. This type of income is generated through various means, such as rental property income, stock dividends, and peer-to-peer lending. Unlike active and passive income, portfolio income is primarily generated from investments and assets rather than personal involvement or effort. On the other hand, passive income is a type of income that generates money with minimal ongoing effort. It is often referred to as "making money while you sleep." Examples of passive income sources include affiliate marketing, ebook publishing, and stock photography. These sources of income allow individuals to earn money even when they are not actively working or putting in continuous effort. In order to generate extra income on the side, there are several ways individuals can explore. These methods can serve as additional sources of income alongside their primary employment or business. Some examples include starting a side business, investing in stocks or real estate, renting out unused space, or taking on freelance or consulting work. These side income opportunities can provide individuals with the chance to increase their overall earnings and financial stability.

There are numerous ways to earn extra money, including engaging in side gigs such as driving for ridesharing services, testing websites, participating in online surveys, and freelancing. You could also start an online business by creating a blog, podcast, or YouTube channel, or by selling digital products such as ebooks, online courses, photography, or music. Additionally, participating in market research studies and focus groups, taking on odd jobs through platforms like TaskRabbit, Fiverr, or Craigslist, or renting out spare rooms, parking spaces, equipment, and other items you own are other options. To effectively build multiple income streams, consider implementing these tips.

To achieve financial success, it's important to start small and slowly build up your income streams. Choose opportunities that align with your skills and passions. Before leaving your primary job, make sure your side incomes are stable. Look into passive and portfolio income streams for the best long-term results. Monitor your progress and income to continuously improve. Reinvest your earnings to expand each income stream. Diversify into various industries to minimize risk. Seek inspiration from successful individuals who have achieved financial success through multiple income streams.

Evaluating the potential success of a business concept is a crucial and initial step when embarking on a new entrepreneurial venture. There are several essential factors that should be carefully considered and examined in order to determine the viability and feasibility of a business idea.

Assessing the market demand is crucial before introducing a product or service in the market. It is essential to conduct extensive market research to have a clear understanding of the target audience and their preferences, needs, and willingness to pay for the product or service being offered. This research will help in identifying gaps in the market and enable the development of a product or service that meets the consumers' demands. Furthermore, understanding market demand will help in developing effective marketing strategies to reach the target audience and promote the product or service in the most efficient manner. Therefore, it is important to conduct thorough market research to determine the market demand, which will ultimately lead to the success of the product or service.

Competition plays a crucial role in analyzing their strengths and weaknesses, enabling businesses to identify distinctive approaches for differentiating their products or services from those of their rivals. By thoroughly studying the competition, companies gain valuable insights that help them formulate effective strategies to stand out in the market. It is essential to thoroughly assess the competition in order to understand their unique selling points and areas where they might be lacking, allowing businesses to capitalize on their own strengths and develop strategies to outperform their competitors. This process involves a comprehensive evaluation of the competition's offerings, market positioning, customer feedback, and overall performance. Through this in-depth analysis, businesses can gain a competitive edge by identifying unmet customer needs, enhancing their value proposition, and creating a unique selling proposition that distinguishes them from the competition. Ultimately, understanding the competition provides businesses with the necessary knowledge and foresight to make informed decisions and successfully position their products or services in the marketplace.

It is important to determine if your business can generate sufficient income to cover expenses and earn profits. To ascertain this, it is crucial to carry out a thorough financial analysis that includes startup costs, operational expenses, and revenue forecasts. This will enable you to determine the feasibility of your business idea and assess its potential for success.

One important factor to consider when evaluating a business is its scalability, which refers to its ability to grow and expand over time. This includes assessing the potential for future expansion, the availability of resources needed to support growth, and the scalability of the business model itself. Essentially, a scalable business is one that can efficiently and effectively increase its operations and revenue without compromising its ability to maintain quality or profitability. As such, scalability is a critical consideration for investors, entrepreneurs, and business leaders who want to ensure long-term success and sustainability for their ventures. Before starting a business, it is essential to investigate any legal or regulatory obstacles that may hinder its establishment. This entails conducting thorough research into the laws and regulations that apply to the industry and ensuring that the business complies with all of them. Failure to comply with legal and regulatory requirements can lead to severe consequences, including fines, sanctions, and even legal action. Therefore, it is crucial to have a clear understanding of the legal and regulatory landscape to avoid any potential obstacles or setbacks. By following all relevant laws and regulations, businesses can establish a strong foundation and build a reputable brand that complies with all necessary legal and regulatory requirements.

Before starting a business, it is essential to assess your own skills and experience to determine if you possess the necessary resources to initiate and manage it. You must critically analyze your strengths and weaknesses and evaluate if you require additional support in terms of employees or partnerships to bridge any gaps. It is crucial to evaluate your abilities and resources to ensure that you can handle the demands of running a business effectively.

In order to decide if a business idea is feasible and worth pursuing, it is essential to assess various aspects. Furthermore, it is crucial to draft a comprehensive business plan that outlines the objectives, approaches, and actions required to initiate and operate the business. This plan can aid in identifying possible hurdles, devising backup plans, and securing funding, if necessary.

# Chapter 4

# Overcoming Financial Obstacles

Having multiple streams of income entails having several different sources of revenue. This method of generating income provides numerous advantages, such as mitigating the risk of financial instability, enhancing the potential to earn more money, and offering a higher level of financial security.

There are numerous ways to generate multiple streams of income. To elaborate, we can take a look at some common examples that people use to diversify their revenue sources. A full-time job offers a consistent and dependable means of financial stability. It ensures a regular flow of income that can be relied upon. With a full-time job, individuals can have a sense of security knowing that they will receive a consistent paycheck, allowing them to meet their financial obligations and plan for the future. This stability also provides a sense of peace of mind, as it eliminates the stress and uncertainty that comes with irregular or fluctuating income. Moreover, a full-time job often comes with benefits such as health insurance, retirement plans, and paid time off, which contribute to a greater sense of financial security and overall well-being. Additionally, having a full-time job can provide a sense of purpose and fulfillment, as individuals can develop and grow in their chosen career path, working towards their professional goals. Overall, a full-time job is not just about earning a living, but it also offers stability, security, and opportunities for personal and professional growth. A side hustle refers to a supplementary job or business that one undertakes in addition to their primary employment. This extra source of income can encompass various activities like freelance work, consulting services, or online product sales.

Investment income refers to the profits generated from various financial instruments such as stocks, bonds, mutual funds, and other forms of investment vehicles.

Rental income is derived from the acquisition and subsequent leasing of real estate properties, such as residential homes or commercial spaces, enabling individuals or businesses to generate revenue through renting out these properties to tenants.

Royalties are the monetary compensation that an individual receives for owning and holding the rights to intellectual property, which can include patents, trademarks, and copyrights. This can be viewed as a form of passive income that is generated from the use of someone else's idea or creation. Essentially, royalties are a legal way of earning money for the use of one's own creative work or invention, allowing the owner to profit from their own ideas and innovations. In today's modern economy, royalties have become a common form of revenue generation for individuals involved in various fields, including music, literature, technology, and more. The amount of royalties received by an individual can vary greatly depending on the specific property and the terms of the agreement with the user.

Overall, royalties serve as a crucial means of compensation for intellectual property owners, allowing them to protect their creations while still receiving financial compensation for their use.

Affiliate marketing is a form of online marketing where individuals promote and advertise products or services belonging to others, and in return, they receive a commission for each sale they successfully generate.

Dividends refer to the financial compensation that a company offers to its shareholders. It is a form of payment made by the company to its investors as a reward for their investment in the business. Such payments are usually made in cash, but they can also be paid in the form of additional shares of the company's stock or other assets. The primary aim of dividends is to provide a return on investment to the shareholders and to foster investor confidence in the company's financial stability and growth prospects. Dividends are often seen as a sign of a company's success and profitability, and they play a crucial role in attracting and retaining investors. In addition, dividends can also provide a steady source of income to investors and help them to meet their financial goals. Overall, dividends are an essential component of corporate finance and a critical factor in determining the value of a company's stock.

Diversifying your income streams is beneficial as it lowers your dependence on a single source of income and opens up opportunities for earning more. It also provides financial stability and flexibility, as it protects you from economic downturns or job loss. Nevertheless, creating multiple streams of income necessitates hard work, commitment, and a willingness to take risks. It is crucial to evaluate each opportunity carefully and ensure that it fits your interests, skills, and financial objectives.

## Chapter 5

## Building a wealth mindset

Developing a mindset focused on building wealth necessitates a deliberate and substantial effort as well as a change in perspective. It involves redirecting attention from instant gratification to long-term financial goals and recognizing the significance of making sound financial choices. Ultimately, cultivating a wealth-oriented mindset is not a single event but a lifelong journey. By staying committed to their financial objectives, making prudent decisions, and continuously learning and evolving, individuals can attain financial success and create a life of abundance. Importantly, fostering a wealth mindset demands an ongoing dedication to personal growth and learning. This may include reading books, attending seminars and workshops, and seeking out new experiences that challenge existing assumptions and expand knowledge. Equally pivotal is surrounding oneself with individuals who possess a positive attitude towards wealth and success. This may involve seeking mentors, networking with like-minded individuals, and avoiding those who hold a negative or limiting outlook on finances. To embark on the journey of building a wealth mindset, it is crucial to establish clear financial goals and formulate a plan to achieve them. This may entail devising a budget, monitoring expenses, and investing in assets that generate passive income. Another crucial aspect of building wealth is cultivating a strong work ethic and a readiness to undertake calculated risks. This may involve pursuing new opportunities, acquiring new skills, and assuming additional responsibilities in one's career or business.

Developing a wealth mindset involves developing a set of attitudes, beliefs, and behaviors that promote financial success and abundance. Here are some strategies for shaping the wealth mindset

Adopting a growth mindset is essential for achieving financial success as it entails the conviction that with dedication and perseverance, one can acquire knowledge and develop skills. This outlook fosters an eagerness to take chances, gain insights from setbacks, and explore novel prospects, all of which are pivotal in building wealth.

Establishing defined financial objectives is crucial as it allows you to concentrate your energy and maintain enthusiasm throughout your financial journey. Moreover, it serves as a comprehensive guide that leads you towards attaining ultimate financial triumph.

It is important to pay attention to the way you talk to yourself, also known as self-talk. Negative self-talk can have a detrimental effect on your self-esteem and drive. However, by monitoring your self-talk and replacing negative thoughts with positive ones, you can cultivate a more optimistic and encouraging mindset.

To develop a positive mindset, it is important to have a supportive circle of individuals around you. This can be achieved by seeking out mentors, coaches, or peers who share similar values and can provide guidance and encouragement. By surrounding yourself with positive influences, you can cultivate a more optimistic outlook on life.

In order to accumulate wealth, it is often necessary to take measured risks. This involves carefully analyzing the potential benefits and drawbacks of each opportunity, enabling you to make informed decisions and pursue new avenues with assurance.

Gaining knowledge from failure is an inherent aspect of the journey towards learning. Rather than fearing or avoiding failure, by embracing it as a chance to gain valuable insights and expand our abilities, we can cultivate resilience and foster a mindset that thrives on growth and development.

Developing a wealth mindset is not an overnight process, but rather requires consistent effort and dedication. To cultivate a positive and forward-thinking mentality, it's important to establish tangible objectives, be mindful of your internal dialogue, and surround yourself with individuals who encourage and uplift you. By embodying these values and practices, you can create a foundation for financial prosperity and abundance.

# Chapter 6

# Conclusion

In order to attain your financial aspirations, it is essential to have a constructive outlook and concentrate on self-improvement. It is crucial to establish precise financial goals and broaden your revenue sources while making prudent financial choices. The process of accumulating wealth is a gradual one and demands commitment, self-control, and endurance. Nevertheless, with a positive attitude and effective tactics, you can formulate a comprehensive blueprint that will guide you towards financial triumph and guarantee a flourishing tomorrow.

www.ingramcontent.com/pod-product-compliance
Lightning Source LLC
Chambersburg PA
CBHW050327220526
45465CB00005B/2168